Home Made Liqueurs

-Recipes for making Liqueurs and Ratafias, Cordials, Shrubs, Brandies, Gins, and Whiskies-

by

Ambrose Heath

British Library Cataloguing-in-Publication Data
A catalogue record for this book is available from
the British Library

Contents

HOME-MADE LIQUEURS

These are still easier to make than wines, since they are merely flavoured spirits requiring nothing more than infusion. Beside the obviously flavoured brandies, gins and whiskies, there are several liqueurs known to our great-grandmothers under various names: the *Ratafias*, which derive their name originally from an almond flavour from the fruit stones; the *Cordials* originally so named, I suppose, from their invigorating effect on the heart; and the *Shrubs*, generally, though not always, made with rum—rather syrupy concoctions warranting a name derived from the Persian for sherbet. Examples of all these will be found in the pages that follow, charming relics of the past centuries that deserve resuscitation.

And indeed I think they are far more deserving of survival than the home-made wines, which, though many will drink them with interest as a curiosity, could never take the place of French and other wines at our tables. But the home-made liqueur, which costs only the merest fraction more than the spirit with which it is made, offers the ambitious host or hostess a chance to exhibit his skill as a blender and to round off a meal with a little something of his own, a pleasant spiritous revival from the days of old and yet as worthy of approval as the conventional liqueurs of which we often get a little tired.

Apricot Ratafia

Cut twenty-five ripe apricots in pieces, break the stones and take out the kernels, blanch these and pound them in a mortar. Put them and the apricots into a jar with half a pound of white sugar, eight cloves, a piece of cinnamon stick and a quart of brandy, cork tightly and leave for three weeks, shaking the jar often meanwhile. Then strain and bottle.

Athole Brose

Mix a pound of run honey into a bowl and add about a teacupful of water to dissolve it. Stir with a silver spoon and, when well mixed, add gradually a pint and a half of Scotch whisky. Stir rapidly until a froth rises, then bottle and keep tightly corked.

Banana Liqueur

Slice some peeled ripe bananas (they must be quite sound and undamaged) and use them to three-parts fill wide-mouthed bottles. Fill up with brandy, and infuse for a month, shaking now and then. Now boil half a pint of water for five minutes with a pound of white sugar, skim it and let it get quite cold. Strain the brandy and after sweetening it to taste with the syrup, bottle.

IMITATION CASSIS

Black Currant Liqueur

Put a quart of sound, ripe, topped-and-tailed black currants into a jar with a pint and a half of brandy, and add a pound of crushed sugar candy and six whole cloves. Cover tightly and, after infusing for three months, filter and bottle.

Four Fruit Ratafia

Take equal quantities of Morello and Duke cherries, red currants and raspberries, all sound and ripe, mash them up separately and then mix them together in an earthenware pan or tub. Leave them there for five hours, stirring now and then, and then press them through a fine sieve. To each pint of this juice allow a pint of brandy and half a pound of white sugar, mix well together and pour into a jar. Cork well and leave for a month, stirring or shaking fairly often meanwhile; then let it stand a while to clear and draw off all the clear liquid. Pass the rest through a jelly-bag, add this to the rest and bottle.

Imitation Cassis

Bruise three-quarters of a pound of sound, ripe black currants, topped and tailed, and put them into a jar with two ounces of raspberries, a single clove, half an inch of cinnamon stick and half a pound of white sugar, and pour a quart of unsweetened gin over them. Leave, covered, for six weeks, then filter and bottle.

Imitation Crème de Menthe

Put a quart of brandy into a jar with six ounces of crushed sugar candy, the strained juice of two lemons and two dozen sprigs of fresh young mint. Leave covered for a fortnight, then filter and bottle.

Imitation Curaçao

Pare the rinds from six Seville oranges and one lemon very thinly, so that there is no pith on it, and put it into a jar with a teaspoonful of coriander seeds, a stick of cinnamon weighing half an ounce, and a pinch of saffron threads. Pour three pints of brandy over these, cork tightly and leave for six weeks in the warm. Then boil two pounds of white sugar with three pints of water, and when cold mix with the brandy which you have filtered through a flannel cloth or jelly-bag. Then bottle.

Lemon Liqueur

Put two bottles of brandy into a jar with a cover, and add three-quarters of a pound of white sugar, the strained juice of eight lemons and the finely-pared rind of them, seeing that it is quite free from the white pith. Pour on to this a quart of boiling milk, stir well together and leave, covered for eight days, stirring every day. Then filter and bottle.

Peach Ratafia

See **Apricot Ratafia** (page 52), using peaches instead.

Quince Liqueur

Peel and grate twelve pounds of ripe quinces into a bowl and sprinkle them with three-quarters of a pound of caster sugar. Leave for twenty-four hours, then strain the juice through a jelly-bag and measure it. To each pint of the juice allow an inch stick of cinnamon, six ounces of white sugar and a pint of whisky. Infuse, closely covered, in a jar for three weeks, then filter and bottle.

Raisin Liqueur

First rub a quarter of a pound of lump sugar on the rind of an orange, and put it into a jar with the strained orange juice, a pound of stoned and chopped raisins, four whole cloves, a quarter of a nutmeg, grated, and a quart of brandy. Infuse tightly corked for a month, and then filter and bottle.

Rowanberry Liqueur

Bruise a pound and three-quarters of ripe mountain ash berries, and put them into a jar with a pound of crushed sugar candy and a quart of whisky. Cork tightly, infuse for three weeks, shaking occasionally, and then filter and bottle.

CORDIALS

Aniseed Cordial

Put an ounce of aniseed and half a pound of white sugar into a quart of brandy, and leave to steep for three weeks. Then filter, and store in airtight bottles.

Blackberry Cordial

Put three quarts of bruised, ripe, sound black-berries into a jar with six ounces of crushed sugar candy, an ounce of bruised root ginger and the thinly-pared rind of a lemon. Pour three pints of whisky over them, cover closely, and leave for three weeks. Then strain and bottle.

Black Currant Cordial

Put a pound of sound, ripe blackberries into a jar with half a pound of finely-crushed sugar candy, and pour in a pint and a half of unsweetened gin. Cork tightly, leave for two months, and then filter and bottle.

Caraway Cordial

Put an ounce of caraway seeds and two ounces of bruised root ginger into a quart of brandy with two ounces of white sugar, and leave covered for ten days. Then filter and bottle.

Cinnamon Cordial

Put six ounces of crushed sugar candy and four ounces of bruised cinnamon stick into a jar with a quart of whisky, and infuse for ten days, shaking the jar frequently. Then filter and bottle.

Clove Cordial

Dissolve half a pound of sugar candy in half a pint of cold water, and put it into a jar with two ounces of cloves, two ounces of coriander seeds, two dozen crushed ripe black cherries and a quart of unsweetened gin. Leave covered for a month, then filter and bottle.

Cranberry Cordial

Make a pint of fresh cranberry juice without any water, and add a pound of white sugar. Stir until dissolved, then add the thinly-pared rind of an orange, an inch of cinnamon stick, six whole cloves and a quart of whisky. Infuse in a tightly corked jar for a month, then strain or filter, and bottle.

Damson Cordial

Have ready some wide-mouthed glass bottles, and half-fill them with sound, ripe damsons, allowing four ounces of crushed sugar candy, a small vanilla pod, two inches of lemon peel and a small piece of cinnamon stick and of root ginger to each pound of the fruit. Fill the bottles up with brandy, and let the contents infuse for six months, tightly corked. Then strain or filter and re-bottle.

Ginger Cordial

Put a quart of rum into a jar with two ounces of crushed root ginger and the thinly-pared rind and strained juice of three lemons, and leave covered closely for a month. Then boil three-quarters of a pound of white sugar with a quarter of a pint of water for ten minutes, skimming as necessary, and when this is cold add the filtered rum to it, and bottle.

Gooseberry Cordial

Put a pint of fresh, ripe gooseberry juice into a jar with a quart of unsweetened gin and add half an inch of bruised cinnamon stick, four cloves, a strip of lemon rind, and three-quarters of a pound of crushed sugar candy. Infuse, covered closely, for a month, shaking the jar now and then, and then filter and bottle.

Highland Cordial

Strip enough white currants to make a pint, and mix them with a bottle of Scotch whisky, a teaspoonful of ginger essence and the thinly-peeled rind of a lemon. Leave for two days, then strain and add a pound of sugar. Leave for another day for the sugar to dissolve completely, and bottle and cork. It can be drunk in three months' time.

Plum Cordial

Weigh some sound, ripe plums, prick them all over with a knitting-needle, and half-fill wide-mouthed glass bottles with them, adding six ounces of crushed sugar candy, four cloves and a half-inch stick of cinnamon to each pound of the plums. Fill the bottles up with unsweetened gin, and leave tightly corked for three months, shaking the bottles occasionally. Then strain or filter and re-bottle.

Raspberry Cordial

See **Blackberry Cordial** on page 56, but use raspberries in place of the blackberries.

SHRUBS

Brandy Shrub

Put the thinly-pared rind of a lemon and the strained juice of two lemons into a jar with a quart of brandy and three-quarters of a pound of white sugar, and leave, covered closely, for five days. Then strain, add a quarter of a small teaspoonful of grated nutmeg and a pint and a half of sweet sherry. Filter and bottle.

Greengage Shrub

Put a pound of sliced sound ripe greengages into a jar with half their kernels, adding half a pound of crushed sugar candy and the thinly-pared rind of half a lemon, and pour over a quart of rum. Cover closely, and leave for six weeks, shaking the jar now and then, and then strain or filter, and bottle.

Mulberry Shrub

See **White Currant Shrub** on page 63, but use mulberries instead of the currants.

Orange Shrub

Boil together for five minutes, skimming when necessary, a pint of strained orange juice and two pounds of white sugar. Let it get cold and then put it into a jar with a quart of rum. Cover tightly and leave for six weeks, shaking the jar twice a day for the first fortnight. Then filter and bottle.

Pineapple Shrub

Cook three pounds of peeled and sliced pine-apple in half a pint of water in a double saucepan for three hours, covered, then strain the juice through a jelly-bag. For each pint of the juice allow six ounces of white sugar and a pint and a half of rum. Mix and stir until the sugar is dissolved, then filter and bottle.

Plum Shrub

Put some pricked, sound, ripe plums into wide-mouthed glass bottles to half-fill them and add, for each pound of the plums, six ounces of white sugar, four plum kernels, and the thinly-pared rind of half a lemon. Fill up with rum, cork tightly and infuse for three months, shaking now and again. Then strain or filter and re-bottle.

Pomegranate Shrub

Rub the pulp of ripe pomegranates through a hair-sieve, measure the juice and to each pint add half a pound of crushed sugar candy, the thinly-pared rind of a lemon, and a quart of rum. Infuse, tightly corked, for a month, then filter and bottle.

Raspberry Shrub

Put two pounds of mashed, sound, ripe raspberries into a jar with the thinly-pared rind and strained juice of a lemon and three-quarters of a pound of white sugar, and pour in a quart of rum. Infuse, tightly corked, for a month, and shake the jar now and again. Then filter and bottle.

Rum Shrub

Pare three lemons thinly, and put the rind into a jar with half a pint of strained lemon juice and a quart of rum. Now boil a pound and a half of white sugar with half a pint of water for ten minutes, skimming, and when this is cold add it to the contents of the jar. Infuse, tightly corked, for a month, shaking it frequently, then filter and bottle.

Strawberry Shrub

See Raspberry Shrub above, using strawberries instead of raspberries.

BRANDIES

White Currant Shrub

Bruise eight pounds of white currants well, sprinkle half a pound of castor sugar over them, and leave until the next day. Then strain the juice and measure it, and put it into a jar with six ounces of crushed sugar candy and a pint of rum for each pint of the juice. Leave covered tightly for two days, then filter and bottle.

BRANDIES

Apricot Brandy

Slice eight sound, ripe apricots and put them into a jar with six of their kernels, a quarter of a pound of crushed sugar candy and a pint and a half of brandy. Cork tightly, and shake every day for a month. Then filter and bottle.

Blackberry Brandy

Bruise a pint and a half of sound, ripe blackberries and put them into a jar with a pint of brandy, a quarter of an ounce of stick cinnamon, three whole cloves and four ounces of crushed sugar candy. Cork tightly and infuse for a fortnight. Then filter and bottle.

Black Currant Brandy

Pick the black currants, sound a ripe, when the sun is hot, and take off the tops and tails. To every three pounds of the fruit add half a pound of white sugar, put them into a jar and fill up with brandy. Cork closely and leave for three weeks, shaking the jar once or twice a day. Then strain and bottle.

Caraway Brandy

Mix two ounces of white sugar with a little ground ginger, and put this with half an ounce of caraway seeds into a pint of brandy. Cork tightly for ten days, then strain through a filter and re-bottle.

Cherry Brandy (Brandied Cherries)

Sound and ripe, but firm, Morello cherries are best for this. Wash and dry them and cut off the stalks, leaving about half an inch on the fruit. Mix them with white sugar in the proportion of a quarter of a pound of sugar to a pound of the prepared cherries, and half-fill wide-mouthed bottles. Fill up with brandy and cork tightly. They should be kept for three months and, if liked, a small piece of cinnamon stick, one or two cloves, and two or three blanched and shredded bitter almonds can be added to each bottle. But they are better plainly made, in my opinion. To serve take out a few cherries with a silver spoon, put them into your glasses and add some of the brandy. The cherries are first eaten, hence the stalks, and the brandy drunk afterwards. The brandy can be made more quickly if the cherries are first pricked all over with a needle, but it is better when they are allowed to remain whole.

Cherry Brandy

Morello cherries are the best for this, and wide-mouthed glass bottles should be half-filled with them, adding ten of the cherry kernels, two whole cloves and three ounces of crushed sugar candy to each pound of the cherries. Fill the bottles up with brandy, cork tightly and leave for three months. Then filter and re-bottle.

Four-Fruit Brandy

Clean and remove the stalks from equal quantities of sound, ripe strawberries, raspberries and cherries, and half the quantity of any one of these of topped-and-tailed black currants. Stew these together very gently, without water and with the lid on until the juice exudes, then strain through a jelly-bag without pressure. When it has finished dripping, measure it, and add to each pint of the juice an ounce of crushed sugar candy or two ounces of Demarara sugar, a few kernels from the cherries, and half a pint of brandy. Leave closely covered for a week or so, then strain and bottle.

Ginger Brandy

Bruise three-quarters of an ounce of root ginger, and put it into a jar with an ounce and a half of white sugar and a pint of brandy. Infuse, tightly corked, for a month, then filter and bottle.

Grape Brandy

Take some sound ripe grapes from their stalks, and three-parts fill wide-mouthed glass bottles with them, adding two ounces of crushed sugar candy to each pound of the fruit. Fill up with brandy, cork tightly and leave for five months, then filter and bottle.

Greengage Brandy

Measure half a gallon of very ripe, but quite sound, greengages, wash and dry them and put them into a pan with only just enough water to cover them. Stir them now and then while they cook gently, and when they are soft, add a pound and a half of white sugar. When this is dissolved and the fruit quite cold, add a quart of brandy, turn into a jar, and leave this, tightly corked, for twelve months, shaking it now and again. The mixture should then be filtered without pressure, and bottled.

Lemon Brandy

This is simple in the extreme. Pare the rinds of four lemons, washed and well dried, as thinly as you possibly can, being careful to avoid all white pith. Put these into a bottle or jar with a pint of brandy, cork well and leave for a fortnight. Then strain and re-bottle.

Mulberry Brandy

Infuse a pint of brandy with a pint of sound, ripe mulberries and three ounces of crushed sugar candy for a month, keeping the jar or bottle well corked. Then strain and bottle.

Orange Brandy

Wash and dry nine Seville oranges, and pare the rinds very thinly without leaving on any of the white pith. Put them into a jar with three pints of brandy, and leave it, tightly corked, for a fortnight. Now make a clear syrup by putting three-quarters of a pound of white sugar into a saucepan with a quart of water and the slightly-beaten white of an egg, and let this boil slowly for an hour, when the liquid should be reduced to about half. Strain this through a fine muslin, and when it is quite cold mix the strained brandy with it, and put in bottles.

Peach Brandy

Cut some sound, ripe peaches into slices with a stainless steel knife, removing the stones, some of which should be cracked and the kernels extracted. Half-fill glass-stoppered jars with the slices, and fill up with brandy, adding two ounces or so of broken sugar candy or rather more Demarara sugar and a few of the kernels to each pint. Screw on the tops and leave for a month, shaking the jars now and then. It is then time to filter the brandy and bottle it.

Pear Brandy

Choose ten large, ripe, juicy dessert pears and peel, core and slice them. Put the slices into a jar with two whole cloves, the thinly-pared rind of half a lemon, half an inch of cinnamon stick, a quarter of a pound of white sugar, and a quart of brandy. Let it infuse, tightly corked, for two months, then filter and bottle.

Pineapple Brandy

Peel a fresh, ripe, undamaged pineapple and cut it in slices or pieces with a silver or stainless steel knife. Put them, after weighing them into glass jars, filling them three parts full and, to each pound of the pineapple allow about half a pound of white sugar, not more, four cloves and two inches of cinammon stick. Fill up the jars with brandy, close down tightly, and after leaving for a couple of months, strain and bottle.

Quince Brandy

Put a pint of fresh quince juice and a pint of brandy into a jar and add six ounces of crushed sugar candy, a very small piece of cinnamon stick and two cloves. Infuse, tightly corked, for two months, shaking now and then; then filter and bottle.

Raspberry Brandy

Put some sound ripe raspberries, picked in the sun, into a double saucepan and let them cook until the juice exudes; then strain this without pressure. Measure it and add half a pound of white sugar for each pint. Boil for three minutes, then skim and, when it is cold, add half a pint of brandy to each pint of the liquid. This can then be bottled.

Raspberry and Red Currant Brandy

Mash equal quantities of sound, ripe raspberries and red currants in a bowl, and let the juice strain through a jelly-bag. Then to each pint of the juice add half a pound of white sugar, let this dissolve completely, and then add half a pint of brandy to each pint of the syrup. Pour into a jar, cover tightly, leave for four or five weeks, and then filter for bottling.

Strawberry Brandy

Three-parts fill wide-mouthed glass bottles with sound, ripe strawberries, add a strip of lemon rind and four ounces of crushed sugar candy to each pound of the strawberries, and fill up with brandy. Infuse, tightly corked, for a month, then filter and bottle.

White Currant Brandy

Put three-quarters of a pound of stripped, sound, ripe white currants into a jar with one or two blanched and shredded bitter almonds, a clove, a very small piece of cinnamon stick and a pint of brandy, cork well down and leave for three months, shaking the jar now and then. After this, filter the brandy and bottle.

GINS

Apricot Gin

Wipe and slice some ripe apricots, removing the stones, and use them to half-fill wide-mouthed glass jars. Add sugar candy or Demerara sugar in the proportion of two ounces to each pound of the fruit and a few blanched and sliced kernals from the stones. Fill the jar up with gin and close them tightly. Leave for three months, shaking now and then, and then strain finely and re-bottle.

Blackberry Gin

Put a quart of ripe, sound blackberries into a jar with half a pound of crushed sugar candy and a pint and a half of unsweetened gin. Cork tightly and leave for three months, shaking the jar each day for the first month. Then filter and bottle.

Black Currant Gin

Pick and top and tail the black currants when they are sound and ripe, and put them into a jar with a wide opening, adding a pint and a half of unsweetened gin and three-quarters of a pound of Demerara sugar to each pound of the currants. Cork tightly, and leave for three months, shaking the jar occasionally. Then strain and bottle.

Cherry Gin

Take the stalks from some sound, ripe cherries, prick them with a needle and half-fill wide-mouthed glass bottles with them, adding six cherry kernels and four ounces of crushed sugar candy to every pound of the fruit. Fill up the bottles with unsweetened gin, cork and seal them and leave them in a cool, dry place for three months, shaking them two or three times a week. Then strain or filter and bottle.

Damson Gin

Make as **Sloe Gin** (page 73), using Damsons.

Lemon Gin

Pare the rinds of four lemons very thinly, and put them into a jar with a quart of unsweetened gin. Cork tightly and leave to infuse for a month. Then strain and add four ounces of crushed sugar candy, leaving again for a week, stirring now and then until the sugar is quite dissolved, then filter and bottle.

Orange Gin

Pare the rinds thinly off three Seville oranges and put them with their strained juice into a jar with a quarter of a pound of crushed sugar candy and a quart of unsweetened gin. Cork tightly, and infuse for three weeks, shaking the jar every day. Then filter and bottle.

Raspberry Gin

Pick over and measure some sound, ripe raspberries, put them into a jar with an equal quantity of unsweetened gin and add one or two ounces of broken sugar candy or a little more Demerara sugar for each quart of the mixture. Cover the jar tightly, leave for a month, shaking the jar every day, then filter carefully and bottle.

Sloe Gin

Quite one of the most delicious home-made liqueurs there is. Prick the ripe sound sloes all over with a needle, and half-fill glass jars with them. Sprinkle on them granulated sugar at the rate of six ounces of sugar to a pound of the prepared fruit, and then cover with sweetened gin, using about a pint and a half for a pound of the fruit. If you use unsweetened gin, double the amount of sugar. Keep tightly corked in a fairly warm place for three months, shaking the jars occasionally, then strain through flannel or filter into bottles and cork tightly. It greatly improves with keeping, and some Cornish friends of mine long ago when gin was half-a-crown a bottle, never drank theirs before it was seven years old, an almost impossible counsel of perfection nowadays.

WHISKIES

Blackberry Whisky

Wash some blackberries, which should be sound and ripe and picked, if possible, on a dry, sunny day, put them as they are into a pan and heat slowly until the juice exudes, but do not let it boil. Then strain through a jelly-bag. Measure the juice, and for each pint add half a pound of white sugar and a muslin bag containing an inch of cinnamon stick, three or four cloves, and the finely-pared rind of a lemon. Boil for half an hour, and when cold take out the muslin bag and add half a pint of whisky to each pint of the juice. When well stirred, bottle and cork down tightly.

Cherry Whisky

Put four pounds of stalked and stoned, ripe, sound cherries into a jar, and add a pound of white sugar, six whole cloves, a quarter of an ounce of bruised cinnamon stick, half an ounce of bruised kernals of the cherries and a quart of whisky. Infuse, tightly corked, for two months, shaking the jar each day, then filter and bottle.

Cranberry Whisky

For a quart of whisky you want a pint of cranberry juice made by stewing the cranberries lightly without any water until the juice has exuded. When it is cold, add the thinly-peeled rind of an orange, and inch of bruised cinnamon stick and half a dozen cloves. Mix with the whisky in a jar, cork tightly and leave for a month. Then strain finely, and bottle.

Ginger Whisky

Bruise three-quarters of an ounce of root ginger and three-quarters of an ounce of dried juniper berries, and put them into a jar with six ounces of crushed sugar candy and a pint of whisky. Infuse, tightly corked, for a fortnight, then filter and bottle.

Lemon Whisky

Infuse a quart of whisky with three-quarters of a pound of crushed sugar candy and the thinly-pared rind and strained juice of four large lemons for a month, keeping the jar tightly corked and shaking it each day, then strain and bottle.

Orange Whisky

See **Lemon Whisky** above, using oranges in place of lemons.

Plum Whisky

Cut some sound, ripe plums in halves, and cook them with their bruised kernels without water in a double saucepan until the juice has exuded. Then strain through a jelly-bag, and to each pint of the juice allow half a pound of white sugar and a pint and a half of whisky. Infuse, tightly corked, in a jar for a fortnight, then filter and bottle.

Raspberry Whisky

Put a pound of ripe, sound raspberries into a bowl, throw over them the very finely grated rinds (no white pith) of an orange and a lemon, and sprinkle them with an ounce of ground ginger. Pour a quart of whisky over them and leave, closely covered, for twenty-four hours.

WHITE CURRANT WHISKY

Strain well and measure, and to each pint add half a pound of white sugar. When this is dissolved and the liquid clear, bottle it.

White Currant Whisky (1)

Pick over a pound of sound, ripe white currants and put them into a bowl with the very thinly-sliced rind of a lemon and an orange, and an ounce of ground ginger sprinkled over them. Add a quart of whisky, cover closely and leave for twenty-four hours. Strain carefully, measure the liquid and add to each pint half a pound of white sugar. Leave again until the sugar is completely dissolved, then bottle it.

White Currant Whisky (2)

Bruise a pound of stripped, sound, ripe white currants, and put them into a jar with three-quarters of a pound of crushed sugar candy, a quarter of an ounce of bruised cinnamon stick, an eighth of an ounce of cloves, a quarter of an ounce of pounded blanched bitter almonds and a quart of whisky. Infuse, tightly corked, for a month, shaking each day, and then filter and bottle.

Lightning Source UK Ltd.
Milton Keynes UK
UKOW041944020413

208568UK00001B/19/P